Young ELi Readers

Jane Cadwallader

Uncle Jack and the Emperor Penguins

Illustrated by Gustavo Mazali

2 Uncle Jack sat in an armchair with May and Daisy and looked at a book about Emperor Penguins. 'Every year the penguins walk many kilometres to the place where they lay their eggs,' read Uncle Jack. The book was by Uncle Peter. Uncle Peter was Uncle Jack's brother and he loved penguins!

The phone started to ring. Jim went to pick it up.

'Hello. Who is it?' he asked. It was Uncle Peter! He was at the Antarctic so it wasn't easy to understand him!

'COME AT ONCE,' shouted Uncle Peter, 'THERE'S A PROBLEM! BRING THE SNOW MAKING MACHINE!'

'We want to come too,' said May and Daisy and Jim. 'O.K.' said Uncle Jack, 'but put on your warmest clothes. It's very cold in the Antarctic!'

The children quickly put on their warmest sweaters and coats and scarves and hats. Of course Grumpy the dog put on his sweater too! Where the children went Grumpy went too!

Uncle Jack gave the snow making machine to Jim and Jim put it into the balloon. 'What a funny machine!' said May, laughing. 'Is it a fan?' 'No,' said Uncle Jack, 'it's a snow making machine.'

The children liked going in Uncle Jack's balloon.
'Oh,' said Daisy, 'there's a jungle!'
'And a mountain,' said May, pointing to a high mountain with snow on the top.
'And an island in the sea,' said Jim.
Uncle Jack pointed in front of them. 'There's the Antarctic. We're nearly there!'

Now Uncle Jack and the children could see the problem! There was a strip of ground which was mud and not snow! The Emperor Penguins couldn't cross. They couldn't walk in the mud!
'Poor penguins!' said Daisy.
'Don't worry!' said Uncle Jack. 'Jim, pass me the snow making machine please.'

The balloon with Uncle Jack and the children flew over the muddy ground. The snow making machine dropped water into the air and the water turned into snow. The ground was white again.
'Hurrah!' shouted May and Daisy happily.
'Hrrrrrrump!' said Grumpy. He was cold and he was NOT enjoying himself.

They said hello to Uncle Peter. He was very different from Uncle Jack. Uncle Jack was tall and thin with straight grey hair, a long nose and glasses. Uncle Peter was short and fat with curly blonde hair and a big beard and moustache.

Uncle Peter was very happy! 'Tomorrow the penguins can go to the place where they lay their eggs,' he said.

Uncle Jack and the children ate supper in Uncle Peter's house. Grumpy watched the penguins from the door. Grumpy didn't like the penguins. His idea was that an animal walked on the ground OR swam in the water. Penguins walked AND swam … Hmmmmmph!

The next day they woke up suddenly. 'What's that?' asked Uncle Peter. Outside the window they could hear men talking.

'Oh! What are they doing? asked Uncle Jack. 'I don't know,' said Uncle Peter, 'but I think it's something bad!'

'Oh no!' said Uncle Jack.
'Now we know why the ground is mud and not ice!' said Uncle Peter.

'Grumpy! Come back! Be quiet!' said Jim … but it was too late. Grumpy ran out of the house and barked at the men. Uncle Jack and Uncle Peter and the children ran out after him.

The men were not happy to see Grumpy. They were not happy to see Uncle Jack, Uncle Peter and the children!

'What are you doing here?' they asked angrily.

'AND YOU?' asked Uncle Peter. 'What are YOU doing here?'

Suddenly they all looked up into the sky. There were two planes.

'Here he comes,' said one of the men.

'Who is HE?' asked Uncle Peter.

The planes landed on the strip of mud. 'Now I understand' said Uncle Jack. 'The strip of mud was for the planes! Planes can't land on ice!' But Uncle Peter wasn't listening. His mouth was open. 'Oh!' he said, pointing to the man in the plane, 'It's Mr Mazzarati!'

'Are you coming to my birthday party?' asked Mr Mazzarati. 'I'm going to be 50 and I want to invite all my friends to a special party here in Antarctica.'
'What? Are you crazy?' Jim asked.
'What about the penguins? They want to go to the place where they lay their eggs!' said May.
'And they can't walk on the mud!' said Daisy.
'They must go NOW!' said Uncle Peter, 'It's getting colder and colder!'

Mr Mazzarati was very surprised. He didn't know about the penguins. But he wasn't a bad man. He wanted to help. Suddenly he had an idea. 'We can take the penguins in the planes!' he said.

The men took the food and drink out of the boxes. There was soup and sandwiches and fruit and cakes and bowls of pasta and lots of sausages! Then the penguins jumped into the boxes.

The planes, with the penguins inside, took off. Uncle Jack and Uncle Peter and the children went with the planes in their balloon. Some penguins had a ride in the balloon too!

Suddenly the penguins were very excited. They pointed down to the ground. 'Oh!' said Uncle Peter, 'Look at the three rocks. That's where the penguins lay their eggs!'

'Goodbye! Goodbye penguins!' shouted May and Daisy. Uncle Peter took photos.

▶ 3 Here are the Emperor Penguins
As happy as can be.
They're off to lay their eggs
In a place far from the sea.

They stay here all the winter
As cold as cold can be.
Until their babies hatch
In a place far from the sea.

4 'Goodbye,' shouted Mr Mazzarati. 'Don't worry! We will tidy up after the party!'

'Goodbye Mr Mazzarati,' shouted the children.

Activity Pages

1 Finish the words. Number the sentences in the order of the story.

◯ Uncle Ja___ and the childr___ went to Antarctica.

◯ They said goodb___.

◯ Mr Mazzara___ landed in a pla___.

① J i m pick e d up the pho n e .

◯ The sn___ maki___ machine made sn___ to cover the grou___.

◯ The plan___ took the pengui___ to the place whe___ they lay their eg___.

◯ They met Unc___ Pet___.

◯ Grumpy r___ out of the hou___ and bark___ at some m___.

2 Match the sentences to make the song.

Here are — the Emperor Penguins
As happy — as can be
They're off — to lay their eggs
In a place — far from the sea
They stay here — all the winter
As cold — as cold can be
Until — their babies hatch
In a place — far from the sea

3 Look at page 2. Write what's missing in this picture.

glasses

4 Find the words. Write them in the correct category.

Food
s o u p
_ _ _ _ _
_ _ _ _ _
_ _ _ _ _
_ _ _ _ _ _ _
_ _ _ _ _ _ _ _

dnalsi
sekac
sevracs
atsap
tiurf

niatnuom   tah

Places
_ _ _ _
_ _ _ _ _ _
_ _ _ _ _ _
_ _ _ _ _ _ _

aes   ~~puos~~

retaews

sehciwdnas

Clothes
_ _ _
_ _ _ _
_ _ _ _ _ _
_ _ _ _ _ _ _

taoc

segasuas   elgnuj

5 Write about Uncle Jack and Uncle Peter.
Use: *He was ...* and *He had ...* .

~~a moustache~~   short   ~~tall~~   a long nose
blonde hair   straight hair   fat   curly hair
grey hair   glasses   a big beard   thin

He was tall.

He had a moustache.

6 Write the missing word.

took   ran   looked   jumped

1 They _____ up at the planes.
2 Grumpy _____ out of the house.
3 The penguins _____ into the boxes.
4 Uncle Peter _____ photos.

7 Imagine you are Jim or Daisy. Draw a picture and write about your adventure with the Emperor Penguins.

8 Do you like the story? Draw your face and choose a sentence to write.

I love it.
I like it.
I quite like it.
I don't like it very much.
I don't like it at all.